the volcano
el volcà

the volcano
el volcà

Poems
Anna Dodas

Translated from Catalan by Clyde Moneyhun
Edited by Ester Pou Jutglar
Afterword by Maria-Mercè Marçal

Francis
Boutle
Publishers

Paisatge amb hivern first published by
Associació de Joves Escriptors, Barcelona, 1986

El volcà first published by
Edicions 62, Provença 278, 08008 Barcelona, 1991

El volcà collected edition published by
La Busca Edicions SL, Castellterçol 3, 0823 Barcelona, 2015

This bilingual edition first published by
Francis Boutle Publishers
272 Alexandra Park Road
London N22 7BG
Tel 020 8889 8087
Email: info@francisboutle.co.uk
www.francisboutle.co.uk

ISBN 978 1 7398955 1 8

CONTENTS

ACKNOWLEDGEMENTS

Anna Dodas i Noguer's first collection of poetry, *Paisatge amb hivern* (*Landscape with Winter*), won the Amadeu Oller Prize in 1985. A member of the jury, Maria-Mercè Marçal, admired the book "*aferrissadament*," and included some of its poems in her anthology of emerging Catalan-language women poets. *Paisatge amb hivern* was republished in 1991 together with a posthumous volume of poetry, *El volcà* (*The Volcano*) and two dozen uncollected poems. It is our honor to offer a translation of that book and to bring Anna's important work to the English-speaking world.

We thank the Dodas i Noguer family for permission to reprint Anna's poetry and publish this bilingual volume, and for their warm support of the project from the beginning. We want to recognize the work of Ramon Farrés, who assembled and edited the original volume. We thank Heura Marçal Serra for permission to translate and include Maria-Mercè Marçal's essay on *The Volcano* as an Afterword. Thanks to *Asymptote Journal*, which published an early version of *Landscape with Winter* on its "Translation Tuesday" blog in Fall 2021. And as always, a thousand thanks to Clive Boutle for making another dream a reality.

Clyde Moneyhun, Maó, Spring 2022
Ester Pou Jutglar, Barcelona, Spring 2022

Introduction

"I have always written. I have short stories written at the age of six", affirmed Anna Dodas in an interview towards the middle of the year 1986. She was then only twenty-three, and had just been awarded the Amadeu Oller Prize for her debut poetry collection, *Paisatge amb hivern* (*Landscape with Winter*, 1986). This was written from her home in Plana de Vic, a fertile inland region with a rural landscape in the northeast of Catalonia, running along the border between the Montseny massif and the foothills of the Pyrenees. Against all expectations, she burst on to the Catalan literary scene through the figure of the feminist poet Maria-Mercè Marçal. As a member of the jury that awarded the prize to Dodas, she declared: "There are poems that I would have liked to have written myself." Unfortunately, Dodas' intense production and blossoming development was tragically cut short when she was brutally murdered whilst travelling with a friend in the south of France in August 1986. Indeed, she had expressed a keen desire to continue writing more.

Anna Dodas Noguer, born in Folgueroles in 1962, graduated from the University of Barcelona with a degree in Catalan Philology. She also attended the Barcelona Conservatory of Music, where she continued her guitar studies and soon performed as a soloist in several towns and cities in Catalonia. She is the author of only two collections of poetry, *Landscape with Winter* and *El volcà* (*The Volcano*), which were posthumously published together in 1991 in a single volume along with a number of uncollected and unpublished poems. In addition to her poetic writing, she also wrote articles and research papers for various journals and magazines, as well as short stories.

There has been growing interest in her work since 2014, when it gained well-deserved recognition through certain events. A recital, "Reivindicació d'Anna Dodas" ("Reclaiming Anna Dodas"), held at the University of Perpignan, and the re-edition of *The Volcano* by La Busca Edicions were crucial to this reconnection. The volume had been out of print for some time and was relaunched with a foreword by Ramon

Farrés, an introduction by Núria Martínez-Vernis and the prologue by Jordi Sarsanedas included in the first publication. For the new edition, a number of reviews appeared in the media; launches and various events were held with a view to further promoting the work and, in 2016, the Barcelona Poetry Festival paid tribute to her. The following year, some of Dodas' poems were included in the anthology *Com elles* (*Like Them*) and the publishing house Sabina brought out *Soy como el trueno / Sóc com el tro* (*I Am Like Thunder*), a translation into Spanish by Max Hidalgo and Caterina Riba of a selection of Dodas' poetry. More recently, Vicenç Altaió and Josep Maria Sala-Valldaura included one of her poems in the volume *Mig segle de poesia catalana* (*Half a Century of Catalan Poetry*), launched in May 2018. Finally, *Capvespres de foc i de grana* (*Sunsets of Fire and of Crimson*, 2018), recovered the writer's fiction for the first time in a book, up to then only appearing in random, diverse magazines or still unpublished.

Writing can be a hostile act, even an aggressive form of expression. Certainly, Dodas' voice is heart-rending, expressing a terrible beauty, filled with pain, yet conveying a challenge. According to Joseph Brodsky, poets should not be viewed through any other prism than that of their poems, meaning that the reader experiences a poem in its own terms. Travelling through Anna Dodas' poetry, you can feel her sorrowful words penetrating your body and shattering your human soul. Her thirteen bare, untitled poems in *Landscape with Winter*, mostly short, cold verses of desolation, evoke sensations of sound and silence, rhythm and symbolism. They project a remarkable feeling of solitude in their condensed lines. The winter season seems only an excuse through which the poet can express her own inner winter. In other words, her own self.

The range of rural lexis used, some original from the so-called Plain of Vic area, is richly sensory and showcases the writer's sensitivity to the local language, closely connected to the land and the community. At times, it mirrors the use of language by the Romantic writer Jacint Verdaguer, from the same hometown as Dodas. Intersections of rural and figurative language come to life, as when she states: "A flock of clouds" or in another poem: "have you seen it, the forest?" which continues later as "there is no memory" / "ni fullaraca" translated as "no fallen leaves". Incorporating metaphors such as the use of the verb "to roar" ("bramar") to refer to the sound of the sea, followed by the verses: "here only the snowy/ crests tucked in/ the fields covered/ with motionless swells", which combine elements that belong to nature and the sea, are clear examples of a fusion of seaside and countryside, real and metaphorical landscapes. In another poem, she makes use of the word "jingling" (Catalan "dringueig"), a localism that alludes to the bell sound produced by a flock of sheep moving around. In the next stanza, the bed becomes "this broad field/ of white sheets" that continues in the final lines by personifying the plain which "makes us long for sleep", and with a closing verse ("while wracked by shivers") that echoes the epigraph from Verdaguer placed at the very beginning of the collection: "The tormented earth groans like a heart".

The second collection that provides the title for this anthology, *The Volcano*, starts with another powerful poem, "I am like the groaning thunder", that speaks for itself. Again, here and throughout the book, the use of punctuation is intentionally sparing, which allows the reader to experience the calm tumult of these poems and the expression of a quiet beauty. Sometimes, this sensation is interrupted by sudden upheaval caused by one or two concise but meaningful words such as night, silences, beyond life, the pain, blood, snow, Death, desolate sorrow, red or in misery, which constitute a whole verse on their own. Occasionally, but clearly conveying Dodas' intentions, these words are even aligned to the right in an attempt to locate them on the margins of the poem.

Besides using a variety of imagery and symbols, thunder alongside fire, trees, cries, red, persistent silences and disturbing solitude, among others, Dodas' real and figurative scenes are also portrayed by using opposite literary motifs (day/night, life/death, masculine/feminine or nature/sea). Throughout these pages, a moaning lyrical voice, an insecure and foolish terror, turns now and then into a rebel voice which rises like fury:

what sucks the white
flower, so it grows so fragile
if not the fire?

In a continuous search for identity, questioning death and fighting res-
ignation to fate. Undoubtedly, the voices of the American poets, Silvia
Plath, Anne Sexton and Emily Dickinson are echoed in Dodas' poems.
For instance, the only poem with a title is 'Father' which takes us
inevitably to the poem 'Daddy' written by Plath. The Catalan poet read
and admired the works of the author from Boston. Beyond the similar-
ity between the titles *Landscape with Winter* and *Winter Trees*, they use
almost identical images to refer to the female, and a poetic voice in the
last lines of "Lady Lazarus" who reminds us of the voice in the last
poem before entering the uncollected poems section. Dodas wrote:

and the slender mountain
all alone and safe
carries thunder in her belly

ABOUT THIS EDITION
This edition includes the translations of all the poems in the La Busca
2015 edition of *El volcà*, retaining the same three sections: *Landscape
with Winter*, *The Volcano*, and the *Uncollected and Unfinished Poems*. Due to
its impelling and symbolic force, we also decided to keep *The Volcano* as
the title of the whole collection. The new Afterword is a translation of
an essay dedicated to Anna Dodas, written by Maria-Mercè Marçal in
1991.

Until now, Anna Dodas' poetry had yet to be published in English
translation. It was high time for her work, so unjustly neglected, to be
brought to life beyond the limits of its native Catalan language. The
poems in the original Catalan, face-to-face with their translations into
English, create a beautiful intercultural dialogue that opens them up to
a wider readership. They are sensitively translated by Clyde Moneyhun
who, while working on this edition, confessed to me that of all his

8

translations he felt that he had put his heart into this one of Anna Dodas' work. His comment reminded me of what Mireille Gansel wrote in *Traduire comme transhumer* (*Translation as Transhumance*): "No word that speaks of what is human is untranslatable." If a poem lives in its language, from now on Anna Dodas' poetry lives in the English language too. And, regardless of whether you read the original or the translation, one certainly has a real feeling of reading about fear, loneliness, pain and the deepest human emotions.

It is an immense privilege for me to present this gifted poet and her poetic writing to the English reader for the first time. My hope is that readers will discover a breath-taking gem within these pages.

Ester Pou Jutglar

TRANSLATOR'S NOTE

The poetic voice of Anna Dodas is instantly recognizable: the terrible urgency, the tumble of hypnotically repeated images, the highly specific vocabulary, often presented in unpunctuated fragments that challenge a reader's ability to make grammatical sense of them and compel several readings to consider various possibilities for meaning. As Ramon Farrés says in a 2016 interview, "All this stuns the reader and causes the lexical elements to come rushing in and work together without wanting to." It is a voice that communicates both pain and wonder, mystery and absolute clarity, love and dread. Its imagery is not metaphorical, but constitutes a completely realized poetic world that is an analogue to the poet's lived experience. What Sylvia Plath, whose collecton *Winter Trees* Dodas had read in Catalan translation, says in a diary entry about that book could easily apply to the aesthetic of Anna Dodas: "… small poems, very physical in the sense that the worlds are bodied forth in my words, not stated in abstractions … Small descriptions where the words have an aura of mystic power …"

Between the first and second collections, there is a darkening of the already bleak imagery with the introduction of more overtly violent vocabulary. If the landscape in the first collection shivers under a blanket of snow, in *The Volcano* the earth threatens to erupt at any time. There is also "Father," which breaks new ground in sound and meaning and uses a less dense concentration of images to sustain a longer poem. Grammar in *The Volcano* is somewhat more comprehensible, and the pulse of repeated phrases turns the voice inward, as if it is talking more to itself than to the reader, turning over ideas, reconsidering thoughts:

> I am like the groaning thunder
> That roars in the valley
> mad with terror
> I am the valley

★★★

I am the dizzying
channel that gushes
water in a magnificent leap

I am the leap

As for the final section of the volume, uncollected and unfinished poems, Ramon Farrés tells us in his introduction to original Catalan version of the book that the first four were cut by the author from *Landscape with Winter*, the next three cut from *The Volcano*. (And in fact a reading of these poems reveals the methods and imagery of the two collections from which they were removed.) The remainder of the poems in the final section were assembled from handwritten pages, some of which had multiple versions and corrections in the poet's hand. These are included because, Farrés says, "apart from their obvious poetic interest, they give an idea of a whole group of images and themes dancing in the head of the writer that she might have elaborated upon later in other works." While life still seems threatened by loneliness and despair in these final poems, here and there nature is not so forbidding, dreams are not nightmares, and there are moments of serene (if exhausted) contemplation rather than dread:

it's raining
on the sleeping garden
the afternoon
is tired
a leaf is caught
among the branches
drops fall
one by one
night falls

and it's raining on the garden
sleeping

In his prologue to the original book, Jordi Sarsanedas addresses Anna Dodas "as a companion, a good companion, in the task, perhaps not entirely useless, of making beautiful objects that add humanizing complexity to the spectacle of the world." The translator's task, one hopes not entirely useless, has been to preserve the beauty of Anna Dodas i Noguer's peerless poetry while preserving her vision of our often lonely, painful, and terrifying lives.

Clyde Moneyhun

the
volcano
el volcà

Paisatge amb hivern

Landscape with Winter

La terra adolorida gemega com un cor. – Verdaguer

1

Baixen els flocs
i es disparen les estrelles
cap a un firmament lletós.
L'embranzida, el sotrac.
El meu cor pertany
a la grapa d'un ogre.
Galopa, galopa
salta
galopa, galopa
les muntanyes com un mar
furient.
Ploren, ploren les
campanes.
Un aixeta degota
com un plor
que rellisca.
Tot dorm.

The tormented earth groans like a heart. – Verdaguer

1

Hair comes undone
and stars shoot
across a milky firmament.
The acceleration, the jolt.
My heart fits
into the paw of an ogre.
Gallop, gallop
jump
gallop, gallop
mountains ferocious
as the sea.
They cry, the bells,
they cry.
A faucet drips
like a streaming
tear.
Everything sleeps.

2

Un ramat de núvols
carreteres blanques
neu, neu, neu.
Sageta de silenci
s'ajeu l'aire quiet.
Muda
        la vida.

Fes-me un lloc, fes-me un lloc
patina tot com una pista
                    de glaç.
No veig res, sóc cega
enlluerna
        reverbera
                la llum.

Neva.
Sacrifica espais
endu-te'n, si pots, la imatge:
res no roman
            res més
que una gran
        desolada tristesa.

2

A flock of clouds
white avenues
snow, snow, snow.
Arrow of silence
flattens the air.
Life itself
          is mute.

Make room for me, make room for me
patina like a track
                    of ice.
I see nothing, I am blind
the light
          dazzles
                    echoes.

It's snowing.
Sacrifice spaces
take away the image, if you can:
nothing remains
                    nothing more
than a vast
          desolate sorrow.

3

has vist el bosc
enllà del riu
freds esquelets de roure?

res no respira
el brancatge arrissat
com un dubte fòssil
res no s'hi mou

com és feixuga
              la tarda
la neu

l'has vist, el bosc?
transfigurat
no hi ha record
ni fullaraca
com l'altre bosc
més enllà de la vida

3

have you seen the forest
past the river
frozen skeletons of oak trees?

nothing breathes
the twisted branches
like a fossil doubt
nothing there moves

how heavy it is
                    the afternoon
the snow

have you seen it, the forest?
transfigured
there is no memory
no fallen leaves
like that other forest
beyond life

4

Cremen endins endins
les llars enceses
profundes.
Aquella tova catifa
vermella taronja
és el foc
            les flames blanques.
Trontollen indecisos els camps
de neu.
Terribles ombres
allargassades
als marges.

4

They burn within within
the homes on fire
in their depths.
This soft carpet
red orange
is the fire
           the white flames.
They stagger indecisive
fields of snow.
Terrifying shadows
stretched
along the edges.

5

S'amaren els vidres
nostàlgia immensa
riu de llàgrimes
finestra

rellisca avall tot
quietament
rodó com el gat
a l'estora

ara els grans vents
avancen
sense remor
pel camí de plomes

S'adorm el cor
i els cristalls xops
les lentes gotes
com s'abalteix
                    el món.

5

The panes are dripping
immense yearning
river of tears
window

streams down
so quietly
round as a cat
on a carpet

now great winds
advance
without a sound
down the street of quills

The heart dozes off
and the crystals drenched
the drops slow
as if the whole world

                    grows drowsy.

6

el riu
el llarg mirall
arbres morts
fredes arrels
Puja i baixa
la saba antiga
dels salzes moribunds

blanques ninotes

qui ve, qui ve
a destorbar
el son?

6

the river
the long mirror
dead trees
cold roots
The ancient sap
of dying willows
rises and falls

white mannequins

who comes, who comes
to trouble
sleep?

7

Es desprèn
un meteor brillant
i lluu l'escorça gelada
de la terra.
Espurnes palpitants
els tènues estels
de la tenebra.
Com un cigró
            un robí
rodola i rodola
pel negre
            pel blanc.
Caldran molts freds
molts més freds
per desfer la mineral duresa
de la sang
            fossilitzada.

7

A brilliant meteor
frees itself
and lights the frozen crust
of the earth.
Pulsating sparks
faint stars
in the darkness.
Like a chickpea
                a ruby
it tumbles over and over
now black
                now white.
They must be very cold
much, much colder
to dissolve the mineral hardness
of fossilized
                blood.

8

traços negríssims
ferides de tinta
                violàcia
un enorme arc
un prisma
arrodoneix el cel
Estrepitoses marees
i un enyor ferotge
On és la calma
l'anhelada promesa?

8

ebony traces
wounds the color
                    violet
an enormous rainbow
a prism
rounds the sky
Thunderous tides
and a fierce longing
Where is the calm
the longed for promise?

9

Vingueren cavalls
amb ulls de maragda.
Un anell verd viu
sorprengué la nit.
La Mort
fornida de sella
i agafat a la crina
l'amor

no caiguis

la cua suau
com fils de seda.

El bosc nocturn
oculta el trepig
angoixant
el clac clac
les petjades
i els renills
                salvatges.

9

Horses came
with eyes of emerald.
A ring vivid green
surprised the night.
Death
strong in the saddle
holding love
by the mane

you musn't drop

the tail as soft
as filaments of silk.

The evening forest
obscures the steps
anguished
the clip clop
the hoofprints
and the wild
                neighing.

10

qui pensa ara en la mar
que deu bramar molt lluny
d'escumes i gavines?
aquí només les crestes
nevades que reposen
els camps colgats
en estàtiques onades

i en la nit constel·lacions
contemplant-se entotsolades

10

who thinks now about the sea
that roars in the distance
with crashing waves and seagulls?
here only the snowy
crests tucked in
the fields covered
with motionless swells

and at night constellations
observe themselves in isolation

11

esmola més la pena encara
de les desertes nits
de neu
aquell dringueig solitari
del trineu errabund
pujolar enllà

els dits gelats de l'hivern
em rellisquen per l'esquena
el llit, aquest gran camp
de llençols blancs

i mentrestant la plana
recorda arços florits
els pètals nivis
l'aroma suau la brisa
i es vol adormissar
mentre tremola agemolida

11

it sharpens all the more the torment
of lonely nights
of snow
this desolate jingling
of a sled wandering
a distant hill

frozen fingers of winter
glide across my back
the bed, this broad field
of white sheets

and meanwhile the plain
remembers flowering hawthorns
the frosty petals
the soft scent of the breeze
and makes us long for sleep
while wracked by shivers

12

vagaregen tristos gossos
l'extensa nit emmantellada
i els blancs fantasmes sotjant
la lenta mort el son pregon
Tot sense ressò sense petjada
ecos somorts la llisa manta
regust suau d'absències colgades
aquell finíssim gust d'eternitat
ancorada en un mar de plata
I la lenta plana a sota
la blana llosa marbre

12

sorrowful dogs wander
the spacious blanketed night
and the watchful white ghosts
the slow death the deep sound
All without resonance without hoofprint
the dying echoes the smooth blanket
mild lingering taste of buried absences
that most delicate taste of eternity
anchored in a silver sea
And the slow plain beneath
the velvety marble slab

13

Es rebolca l'albada
retruny de trons.
Sona, ressona
per carrers balbs.
La llum s'hi vessa
amb tota la pena.

Des de quan
            els ocells
són orbs?

Folgueroles, gener-agost 1985

13

Dawn rolls over
rumble of thunder.
It sounds, resounds
in the numb streets.
The light spills into them
with all its pain.

When did
        the birds
go blind?

Folgueroles, January-August 1985

El volcà

The Volcano

I

sóc com el tro
gemegós que braola en la vall
foll de terror
jo sóc la vall

com al rampí
cec entre pedres
que ensopega amb al terròs

sóc la foradada
vertiginosa que escup
aigua en un salt magnífic

jo sóc el salt

no sóc res més:
una carolina molla
que aguanta la pluja
                    tristament

I

I am like the groaning thunder
that roars in the valley
mad with terror
I am the valley

like the rake
blind among the rocks
that stumbles on a clod of earth

I am the dizzying
channel that gushes
water in a magnificent leap

I am the leap

I am nothing more:
a wet poplar
that endures the rain
                              in misery

l'incendi s'apropa
cendres cortines de fum
bafarades d'escalfor
l'incendi s'apropa i els merlets
buits les torrasses soles
l'incendi, la por
cavalls que s'escapen

the fires draw near
ashes curtains of smoke
stench of heat
the fires draw near and the battlements
empty the towers alone
the fires, the fear
the horses that flee

immòbils des de temps immemorials
crespuscles encesos
vena oberta, vísceres, cavernes
el vermell que tot ho rega
silencis

dos sols surant per calitges
talment dos cors

motionless from time immemorial
twilights ablaze
open vein, viscera, caverns
the red that soaks everything
silences

two suns floating in the haze
just like two hearts

el fred altiplà de gel
la seda taronja suaument onejada
el bleix tenebrós de la mar gegantina
fumeroles negres cap al bronze del cel

parlar d'amor, encara
i un saxo es manté
esgarrapant contra la nit

the cold plateau of ice
orange silk gently waving
the dark panting of a gigantic sea
black clouds of smoke up to a bronze sky

speaking of love, still
and a sax keeps it up
scraping against the night

res com un foc, com la brasa
i la mà que l'agafa i es crema
el dolor
i no pas l'agònica successió
de flames i dies
                    incombustibles
i un aire inflamat a dins
la perversa impotència
d'un fat que no és sinó espera

nothing like fire, like the ember
and the hand that holds it and is burned
the pain
and not the agonizing succession
of flames and incombustible
                              days
and air burning from within
the perverse powerlessness
of a fate that holds nothing but waiting

II

aquesta és l'hora quieta de les aus
l'hora dels arbres
i aquests els plans paisatges somnolents
de l'astre errant
              i solitari
els aqüeductes estan quiets i quietes són
les aigües
aquestes les piscines i ningú
per a banyar-se

refila inquiet un clarinet
immers al negre abisme dels ocells
i l'hora

II

this is the still hour of birds
the hour of trees
and these the plains sleeping landscapes
of the star wandering
                           and solitary
the aqueducts are still and still are
the waters
these pools and nobody
to bathe in them

a restless clarinet trills
immersed in the black abyss of birds
and the hour

darrera les muntanyes, agotnades,
hi ha les nits
a punt per a saltar cimeres
abocar-se, vessar-se per la vall
fins a llepar els peus de la casa

se sent ja la remor trepidant
rodolen els rocs per pedreres
feréstega, la nit comença
la seva venjança

behind the mountains, concealed,
await the nights
ready to leap over summits
to pour themselves, spill into the valley
until they lick the feet of the house

already heard the shuddering rumble
the rocks rolling in the quarries
ferocious, the night launches
its revenge

hi ha ombres en la nit
ombres com tinta
taques
també hi ha llums
estels i ulls com flames

tremola el gos, les velles ruïnes
del castell i arbredes mortes
després, els llargs carrers
i blancs camins lligant-se

la nit respira, i és l'aire fred
el que m'abraça

there are shadows in the night
shadows like ink
stains
also there are lights
stars and eyes like flames

the dog trembles, the ancient ruins
of the castle and the dead groves
later, the long streets
and white roads are joined

the night breathes, and the cold air
is what embraces me

xerriquen amb un so agut
les complicades maquinàries celestes
mil estrelles que giren
dolorosament

les terrasses són buides
i cau una pluja fina
de polsim blanc:
pols d'ossos, d'estels i de néctar

they grind with a high shriek
the complicated celestial machinations
a thousand stars spinning
in misery

the terraces are empty
and a fine rain of white powder
is falling:
the dust of bones, of stars, of nectar

res no sap
la terrible solitud del mussol
udolant per a ningú
aquesta nit sense estrelles
ni el fred la humitat
sota la closca de l'escarbat
en el cau de pudentes plomes

surt una lluna radiant
grassa i fàtua
els grans núvols de la nit corren
a tapar-la

he knows nothing
the terrible solitude of the owl
screeching for nobody
this night without stars
without cold the dampness
under the beetle's shell
in the lair of stinking feathers

a radiant moon rises
fat and vain
the great clouds of night race
to cover it up

aquesta és la nit que les llunes es giren
i mostren terrorífics xucladors
boques badades sense llavis
aquesta és la nit dels rius sagnants
de llargues ombres, de focs apagats
és la nit de carbons, d'espills
sense imatge
una nit sola, espessa
que lentament es podreix

this is the night when moons gyrate
and terrifying blood suckers show themselves
gaping mouths with no lips
this is the night of rivers bleeding
of long shadows, of extinguished fires
the night of coal, of mirrors
without reflections
one night alone, thick
that slowly decomposes

III

la inquietant remor de mil peus
menuts acostant-se
el múltiple ull de la nit, immensa
mosca que et mira
el silenci dens i la sospita
de passes que creixen
d'algues vives alçant-se
sota els peus
l'aire sufocant, ple de perfums
i papallons contra els vidres

petaran les finestres, petaran
les portes
i l'Àngel paorós entrarà
batec de plomes blanques
d'un moment a l'altre

III

the disquieting murmur of a thousand tiny feet
drawing nearer
the compound eye of night, an immense
fly watching you
the thick silence, the suspense
of steps multiplying
of living seaweed growing
under the feet
the suffocating air, full of perfume
and butterflies against the panes

crashing against the windows, crashing
against the doors
and the terrifying Angel will enter
at any moment
beating its white feathers

les venes treballosament empenyen
una sang vermella i espessa
lenta
segueixen els miners
les vetes d'hulla i la pols
per dins les mines

al fons del laberint
en cavernes d'altes sines
se sent glatir el Gran Cor
el cor de pedra de la terra

veins laboriously push
blood, scarlet and thick
slow
miners follow
seams of coal and dust
down the mines

in the depths of the labyrinth
in high caverns of the breast
the Great Heart screams
earth's stony heart

els focs d'artifici esperen
comprimits en els cartutxos
fatalment, la teva ombra rellisca
pels carrers humits
espeteguen en un cel rosat
vàcues llumetes, felices
la teva ombra s'arrossega
per l'empedrat

un llit de plomes, llot
al fons del dòcil riu
meandre
què fóra més plaent que una
barca menada per una gran mà
que la pell d'un xai, la neu
per enfonsar-hi els dits
que les ales fulgurants
d'un àngel mort o que el sexe
humit, bosc emboirat?

the fireworks wait
compressed in cartridges
fatally, your shadow slips
along damp streets
crackling in a rosy sky
empty lanterns, happy
your shadow drags itself
over the pavement

a bed of feathers, mud
in the depths of a river
meanders
what was more pleasant than
a boat steered by a big hand
than the skin of a lamb, snow
to sink the fingers in
than the dazzling wings
of a dead angel or a damp
sex, misty forest?

fuig-me fuig-me cavall
espectre de cavall esquelet
carronya
duel a mort d'escorpins
xarols sobre la pedra calenta
verds verins i sabes mortals
dalles
arreu els rostolls dels blats segats
maregen les cigales maregen les onades
de calor

i tanmateix la nit, el record de la nit
alleugereix l'estrident angúnia dels ocells
del bosc abrusat
de les enceses entranyes esventrades
el cavall mort al mig dels
terrossos
      i el desfici de la mosques

get away from me get away horse
spectral skeleton of a horse
carrion
scorpions' duel to the death
lacquers on the warm rock
poisonous plants and deadly saps
scythes
everywhere stubble of mown wheat
the cicadas are dazed, dazed the waves
of heat

and yet night, the memory of night
alleviates the grating torment of the birds
of the scorched forest
of burning disemboweled entrails
the dead horse lying
on plowed earth
                    and the anxiety of the flies

no és aigua, no, que és el foc
i el mantell argentat és de porpra
no són brises suaus, són remolins
uns llavis vermells de dents esmolades
filera de dents dures i blanques
un sexe ardent on tot s'hi fon
flor de cactus
flor de carn
caòtics plenilunis estivals
repic incontrolat de campanes, insectes
agulles roents

això i no allò altre:
una fossa madura i la terra negra
no hi ha estels en la nit, hi ha
rabents cometes

it is not water, no, it is fire
and the silvered cloak is dyed purple
they are not soft breezes, they are whirlpools
red lips with sharpened teeth
a row of hard white teeth
a burning sex where everything melts
a cactus flower
a flower of flesh
chaotic summer full moons
uncontrolled chiming of bells, insects
white hot needles

this and not that other:
a ready grave and the black earth
there are no stars in the night, there are
speeding comets

al meu pare

darrera l'arc
darrera de la porta
oh pare que hi camines,
què hi ha?
què hi ha en el sord reialme?
els prats, com hi són? cendres?
els lívids camins i solitaris,
cap a quins rius de laves menen?
i el cuc urent devorant budells
hi és de seguida o ve després?
quant triga?
quin aire asfixiant respires, pare,
darrera de la porta?

gegantins tentacles es remouen
al llindar de la Gran Ombra
lassos, els records s'abandonen en la nit oval
l'oblit, el germà gran de grosses mans
de mans peludes
           acollidorament grosses i peludes
què hi ha dins les closes flors nocturnes?
enormes papallones d'ales transparents
fresc silenci tota les mongeteres plenes sota
llampecs d'or creuant l'espai
               inofensius
i el rat-penat vingut de nits estranyes
circumvola hipnòticament el mateix fanal
com si li anés la vida

to my father

behind the arch
behind the door
oh father where you walk,
what is there?
what is there in the hushed kingdom?
the fields, what are they like? cinders?
the ashen solitary streets,
to what rivers of lava do they lead?
and the burning worm devouring the intestines
does it come right away or later?
how long does it take?
what suffocating air do you breathe, father,
behind the door?

huge tentacles move
to the threshold of the Great Shadow
exhausted, memories are abandoned in the oval night
forgetting, the big brother with huge hands
with hairy hands
                          welcomingly big and hairy
what is there in the night's walled-in flowers?
enormous butterflies with transparent wings
fresh silence the bean plants all under
the flashes of gold cruising space
                                            harmless
and the bat arrived from strange nights
hypnotically circles the same street light
as if it were life

PARE

el camí de fum que es dissol tot d'una
o l'ampla mar sense camins
que cal seguir fins a un horitzó
que és un abisme

veus? i ja ets al final
sota l'escorça de l'arbre
la tendresa humida del tronc
el veritable
i darrera l'espessa cortina
una nit profunda de cristall
llarga, llarga, més que el mar
la nova mar que t'espera
quan la mà apartarà el vellut
i davant teu serà la fosca

★　★

s'ha fos
la darrera gota d'aigua
ara el marbre és blanc
com la teva ment tranquil·la
alguna cosa diu, alguna cosa
murmura
i no sents res, ets absent
només el marbre llis i blanc
i la teva ment, callada

★　★

FATHER

the path of smoke that suddenly dissolves
or the wide trackless sea
that you must follow to the horizon
which is an abyss

you see? and now you're at the end
under the bark of a tree
the moist tenderness of a trunk
the real thing
and behind the heavy curtain
a deep crystal night
long, long, longer than the sea
the new sea that waits for you
when your hand parts the velvet
and before you will be darkness

★   ★

it's vanished
the last drop of water
now the marble is blank
like your tranquil mind
something speaks, something
whispers
and you hear nothing, you're absent
only the marble smooth and blank
and your mind, hushed

★   ★

79

si no fos l'espant si no fos la por
trepitjaries ara la catifa blana
segur, tranquil, segur
i fresc en la nova cambra

series
radiant i pur com l'arcàngel
una figura de fum i no pas
groc com una flor com ets ara

i tornaries a ser el d'abans
la suau transparència de l'infant
no nat encara
l'abandó del son en la nit
o la tendresa, l'abraç
d'un pare que no fores

que no fores res més
que la sabata negra i jo a dins
que la soga de la corbata
sempre amb por de morir-hi
que l'estiu de persianes abaixades
una mà groga com un gira-sol
i una mirada de finestra que es bada

series ara, però, la melosa frescor
d'una nit estival, la presència
més enllà del somni, del gemec
del plaer i la tristesa
series el far que giravolta
o el cap molsós endinsant-se
enorme en les aigües

if there were no fright if there were no fear
you would tread the carpet softly
secure, tranquil, secure
and refreshed in the new room

you would be
radiant and pure as an archangel
a figure of smoke and not
yellow like a flower like you are now

and you would again be as before
the soft transparency of an infant
not yet born
the helplessness of a sound in the night
or the tenderness of an embrace
of the father you were not

no more than you ever were
than a black shoe and me inside
than the rope of a necktie
always afraid to die
than summer with the blinds pulled down
a hand yellow as a sunflower
and a look from an open window

now you would be, however, the honeyed freshness
of a summer night, the distant
presence of a dream, of the moan
of pleasure and misery
you would be the revolving lighthouse
or the mossy cape thrusting itself
huge in the waters

i no el gust de bilis
la porta tancada
i la corbata balancejant
sense esma ni esperança

★ ★

vaig a dir-te
el cactus bonyegut i l'aspresa
de l'aire calent de migdia
sorra a la sabata
tu, tovament i suat,
què rumies ara? en qui no penses?
en mi?
penses en mi, ara?
mai no m'has dit
el suau vellut d'un pètal, la brisa
salada d'un mar tranquil
la pluja que embolcalla

i malgrat tot, només et tinc a tu
erecte i poderós com una illa
en l'oceà enfollit que brama

★ ★

fes-te ençà i respira
obre els ulls i mira'm: sóc jo
retorna'm la mà que et vaig deixar
i que ara tens a l'armari
no t'enduguis el cor
el meu cor vermell a la grapa

and not the taste of bile
the closed door
and the necktie swinging
without resolve or hope

★ ★

I'm going to tell you
the swollen cactus and the abrasiveness
of the warm midday air
sand in your shoes
you, soft and sweaty,
what are you pondering now? who not thinking about?
about me?
are you thinking about me, now?
you've never told me
the soft velvet of a petal, the salty
breeze of a tranquil sea
the rain that envelops

and despite everything, I have only you
upright and powerful as an island
in a mad bellowing ocean

★ ★

be here now and breathe
open your eyes and look at me: I am me
give me back the hand I left to you
that you keep in the cupboard
don't carry away my heart
my red heart in your paw

retorna'm l'oreneta envescada
i blava

obre'm la porta que no grinyola
i no siguis el d'ara
obre i digues: «aquí»
seré un cor palpitant i rogenc
a punta d'albada
quan entris, em miris
                i desapareguis

★ ★

ara no és ara ni és un dia
ara ets tu i el matí
serà altra volta Temps

et sé
desinflat com un globus
et sé en la trampa
menut com l'herba menuda
i espantat en la gran prada

sí, i tu no hi ets, mai no hi eres
com un reflex còncau i amenaçant
seràs vano, no pas pols
no cendra, seràs vas i aigua

i per a tu – ara tampoc – serà ara
i el matí no serà matí
i continuaràs sense saber
que jo hi sóc, aquí, asseguda

give me back the swallow
ensnared and blue

open the door that doesn't creak
and don't be who you are now
open it and say: "here"
there will be a beating red heart
at the break of dawn
when you enter, see me

                              and disappear

★   ★

now is not now is not a day
now you are and the morning
will once more be Time

I know you
deflated like a balloon
I know you in the trap
small like a small blade of grass
and frightened in a big meadow

yes, and you're not here, you never were
like a menacing concave reflection
you will be the fan, not the dust
not the cinder, you will be glass and water

and for you – even now – now you will be
the morning and not the morning
and you will continue not to know
that I am here, here, seated

en un moment semblant als teus
però amb tristesa

★ ★

finalment, el mot
tampoc ara no puc dir-te'l
perquè no hi ets
– com abans no hi eres

i doncs, què? la mirada?
el teu ull es belluga encara
però com l'ull del gos
moribund que no comprèn

comprens tu, potser,
que sóc com l'arbre solitari
com el primer estel, estupefacte
com la nota sostinguda com tu
petita i indefensa en aquest erm
en què em deixares?

juliol 86

in a moment much like yours
but with sadness

*   *

finally, the word
I still can't say to you
because you're not here
– as before you weren't here

and so, what? the look?
your eye is still moving
but like the eye of a dying dog
that doesn't understand

do you understand, maybe,
that I am like a solitary tree
like the first star, stupefied
like a sharp note like you
small and defenseless in this wasteland
where you left me?

July 86

IV

saps què s'amaga
sota el pacífic verd
vellutat d'arbres?
                                el roig

què xucla la blanca
flor, per créixer tan fràgil
si no és el foc?

i la muntanya esvelta
tota sola i segura
té a la panxa el tro

IV

do you know what hides
under the peaceful velvety
green of the trees?

                    red

what sucks the white
flower, so it grows so fragile
if not the fire?

and the slender mountain
all alone and safe
carries thunder in her belly

Poemes esparsos i esbossos

Uncollected and Unfinished Poems

1

el perfil de les muntanyes
paper encolat
la neu-escuma que tot ho cobreix
el confetti
xiulen rars vents a fora
del cel pengen cordes immòbils
tot tan buit
tan estranyament abandonat
ningú, ningú hi ha
assegut que miri
aquest tros de no-res
el cartró dels arbres nus
la purpurina daurada
d'una blava nit d'estrelles
tan solitària aquesta nit
la lluna balancejant
al bell mig de l'escenari

1

the profile of the mountains
paper cutouts
snow-foam covering everything
confetti
strange winds whistle outside
from the sky hang motionless cords
all so empty
so strangely abandoned
nobody, nobody here
seated to see
this bit of nothingness
the cardboard of the naked trees
the gilded glitter
of a blue night of stars
a night so alone
the moon rocking
in the center of the scene

2

Digues un nom
el fred, el fred
rellisca tot
      de gel
Només hi ha noms
de vellut negre
capseta de miralls
negra de dins
de vellut negre el dins
confortable

Els grans mantells da la nit

Només l'hivern
desert d'arenes blanques
a coll
Crepiten les neus
a fora

Escolta els crits agònics

I el Silenci

El
gran
plor
del
món

2

Say a name
the cold, the cold
everything slides
                    on ice
There are only names
of black velvet
chest of mirrors
black inside
the inside black velvet
inviting

The great cloaks of night

Only winter
desert of white sands
in your arms
The snows crackle
outside

Hear the dying screams

And the Silence

The
great
sob
of
the world

3

irisacions inconsistències

neu
l'afany, el neguit
arbres pelats
brancatge, pena
desolació hibernal
letargia
segur catau
el refugi oh el refugi
l'ansiat
on va el riu el riu que
no duu enlloc
el riu d'hivern

circulars tristors
cada any cada any
com salten obstacles
els cavalls els meus
cavalls
els ulls-miratge
i les muntanyes
                    ertes
tan lluny tan lluny
és tot tan lluny
com la màgica paraula
un nom
I tot recomença:
el sol hipnòtic
estúpides estrelles
                    fosforescents

3

iridescences inconsistencies

snow
the effort, the anguish
barren trees
branches, grief
winter desolation
lethargy
safe shelter
the refuge, oh the reuge
the anxiety
where does the river go the river that
carries us nowhere
the river of winter

recurring miseries
every year every year
like horses jump obstacles
my horses
horses
the mirage-eyes
and the mountains
                        upright
so far so far
it's all so far
like a magic word
a name
And it all starts over:
hypnotic sun
stupid stars
                        phosphorescent

la terra balba
abandonats carrers
i els empedrats.
Tot recomença
i el fred persisteix

numb earth
abandoned streets
and pavements
It all starts over
and the cold persists

4

Processó d'escarbats
desgranat rosari
de paraules
joc inúitil
el llarg
hivern
l'hivern
de sempre

4

Procession of beetles
fingered rosary
of words
useless game
the long
winter
winter
as always

5

sóc de vidre
una bombolla de vidre amb braços
i cor
vidre trencadís
i a dintre res

a dintre quan es trenqui
un aire
un vent calent, un vent
de sorra
            esgarrifós

5

I'm made of glass
a glass bubble of arms
and a heart
breakable glass
and nothing inside

inside when it's broken
a gust
a warm wind, a wind
of horrifying
         sand

6

qui diu la mort? és l'amor
aquella dama de l'eina negra,
no és la mort ni l'amor
ni hi ha dama i res no du

són les ombres escapadisses
dels astres, de la nit
i de les pors res no en saben,
mentre pasturen plàcids,
negres cavalls els prats veïns

6

who says death? it's love
that lady with the black tool
it's not death and not love
nor is there a lady and she carries nothing

they're shadows escaped
from stars, from the night
and they know nothing of fear
while placid black horses graze
in neighboring pastures

7

mentre dura no faig sinó veure
madures cireres de polpa carnosa
s'aixequen vapors vegetals
                    asfixiants
roses reblanides, boes en combat
una mà enguantada es fica en el llot
llunyà, el sotragueig del tramvia sotragueig
de l'insecte damunt el lilà
teixit d'arrels i ceres foses

l'aire vivificant després
aigües pesants que inunden per dins
els membres i els ulls
creixen pertot llessamins
i densos licors
                    gelatines

7

while it lasts I do nothing but see
ripe cherries with fleshy pulp
plant vapors arise
                    suffocating
softened roses, battling boas
a gloved hand pushed into mud
far away, the bump of a tram bump
of an insect on a lily
woven from roots and melted wax

after life-giving air
heavy waters that flood
through limbs and eyes
jasmine growing everywhere
and thick sticky
                    liqueurs

8

rellisca d'entre els dits l'anguila
llisca la serp com l'aigua
i tot es contorsiona sagaçment
a sota l'aigua

a sota el pont abandonat
viuen els peixos i les pedres
mercuris i maragdes
cada fulla sap com llisca
la gota d'aigua
i cau a l'aigua

el teu cos com un peix d'or
i dintre el riu
                les aigües

8

the eel slips between fingers
the snake slides like water
and all wisely coil
under the water

under the abandoned bridge
fish live and stones
mercuries and emeralds
every leaf knows how
the drop of water slides
and falls into the water

your body like a golden fish
and within the river
                    the waters

9

els sorolls de la nit
                    o silencis
les altes hores passen
res més que el silenci i un foc
sota cendres llunyanes
el matí serà rosa
ara és blanc i cansat
sota silencis de palla

Tu fores silenci i ara ets
espina

9

sounds of night
                or silences
the late hours pass
nothing but silence and a fire
under the distant cinders
morning will be pink
now it's white and tired
under silences of straw

You were silence and now you are
a thorn

10

si veiessis
la grapa de la nit com s'acosta
el fred contacte
si veiessis l'escarbat cec
i el jardí clos com una tanca
les finestres, finestres barrades
el xiprer encarcarat com els segles
com una carcassa
si veiessis la foscor
la silueta de la cases
i espectres que hi vaguen

jo sé l'esquelet del gos
l'eterna cançó noctàmbula
i fa por, fa por la casa
voltada de fulles i troncs
que raspen
jo només sé la nit
i la gran mà que es tanca

10

if you saw
how night's claw approaches
the cold contact
if you saw the blind beetle
and the garden shut like a barricade
the windows, windows barred
the cypress stiff as the centuries
as a carcass
if you saw the darkness
the silhouette of the houses
the ghosts that wander there

I know the dog's skeleton
the endless sleepwalking song
frightened, the house is frightened
surrounded by leaves and branches
that scrape
I know only the night
and the big closed hand

11

Vam ser de plata un dia
o una nit
sí, una nit de metalls
que brunyia l'escorça
de tot
Els cossos inerts
el fred argentat
el silenci brillant
i fi com una espasa
Un bany platejat
damunt la pell insensible
metàl·lics, ben metàl·lics
Com era tot de mineral
aquella lluna de llautó
l'aram de les muntanyes
la glaçada lluïssor
de la nit
I tots els membres erts
de plata
els ulls de plata, la pell de
plata, de plata el dolorós respir
i el sentir
plantejades les ombres lluents
i les veus tancades en una gorja
esdevinguda d'argent
Ben quiets
escoltant el fòssil silenci
d'aquella nit morta,
recordes,
la nit de freds miralls
aquella nit
       metàl·lica.

11

We were silver one day
or one night
yes, a night of metals
that polished the surface
of everything
The motionless bodies
the silvered cold
the silence glittering
and sharp as a sword
A silver-plated bath
under the numb skin
metallic, all metallic
Like everything was mineral
this moon of brass
these copper mountains
the frozen glitter
of the night
And all the straight limbs
of silver
eyes of silver, skin
of silver, silver all the painful breaths
and feelings
the grieving glowing shadows
and the strangled voice of a throat
become silver
So quiet
listening to the fossil silence
of this mortal night,
remember,
the night of cold mirrors,
this metallic
                    night.

12

Hi hagueren llampecs i calors
un dia, qui sap quan
Res més, la lenta bola creix
Se'n van els gitanos
amb els estris de fer música
i el prat, desert,
assenyala la blanca fugida

On és aquell trist desig
on és la sòlida calma
te'n vas, ho sé prou bé
i res no es cansa de repetir-ho
La lenta vida, aquell somieig

12

There were lightning and heat
one day, who knows when
Nothing more, the slow ball grows
The gypsies are leaving
with their musical instruments
and the meadow, deserted,
reveals their empty flight

Where is that sad desire
where is the solid calm
you're leaving, I know that well enough
and repeating it never gets old
Slow life, that dream

13

a dalt de l'espadat
aquell penyal a punt de caure
jeuen els cossos inerts
sobre les sorres blanques
erectes atzavares
cap a un cel absent
i desencuriosit
amples mars
planes mars i amples
fressades sense camins
tu no hi ets tu ho hi ets
només la via solitària
travessa les platges
amb fulgors desesperats

13

at the edge of the cliff
the boulder about to fall
motionless bodies lie
on the white sands
agaves straight up
to a sky absent
and incurious
wide seas
seas flat and wide
well-traveled with no path
you're not there you're not there
only a solitary track
crosses the beaches
with desperate flashes

14

és ara que tomba el llustre sagnant
que tot reposa i s'estira el silenci
la negra ploma
que els borinots i les motos i llum
ja no brunzeixen
és ara que la nit molla ens penetra
que sento que han d'arribar caravanes
els gitanos
       cada estiu
            caravanes
s'encendran els focs i els mussols udolen
s'encendran focs, i jo els veuré
els seus cavalls
suats
entre les flames

14

it's now the bloody luster falls
now that all rests and the silence stretches out
the black feather
now that the bumblebees and motorbikes and light
no longer buzz
it's now the damp night penetrates
when I hear the caravans have arrived
the gypsies
                every summer
                            caravans
fires are lit and owls screech
fires are lit, and I see them
their horses
sweating
among the flames

15

l'entrada de casa és
un prodigi de focs de sant joan
les flames esvalotades brases
amargants
i els papallons de la nit
morent translúcids en el fum
els meus cabells elèctrics
el meu cos crepitant
                com un abre
negres homes atien la fúria

i jo que no puc passer
la son – el llit tan lluny –
que em fa caure a la calenta
abraçada

15

the door into the house is
a marvel of the fires of saint john
the flames embers in turmoil
bitter
the night moths dying
translucent in the smoke
my tresses electric
my body crackling
                    like a tree
black men stirring up the fury

and I who cannot cross over
 the sleep – the bed so far away –
that makes me fall into a warm
embrace

16

aquest ull a l'estesa cua del paó
aquest ull negre immòbil
ple i rodó
trist ull plantat enmig la seda
                          el borrissol
on l'he vist, on l'he vist
en quina cara desesperant mirava
aquest ull insistentment
quasi diria
            que amb dolor?

16

this eye in the spread tail of the peacock
this black motionless eye
full and round
sad eye planted in the middle of the silk
                                    the down
where did I see it, where did I see it
in what despairing face did I look
this eye insistent
I would almost say
                    as if in pain?

17

brunzeix el borinot somnolent
els vidres resseguint una i altra volta

                      sense memòria

brunzeix ardent l'aire
un eixam d'insectes rabiós

17

the drowzy bumblebee buzzes
returning to the window over and over

                                    without remembering

the warm air buzzes
a swarm of rabid insects

18

algú inventa, algú inventa
aquest mar de plata fosa
el vent de ponent que assota la ciutat

18

someone invents, someone invents
this sea of molten silver
the west wind that lashes the city

19

han marxat els cavalls al galop
dies ha que nerviüts s'enlairaven
han marxat primer un després tots
i la prada aixafada, al llot peülles
marcades, el riu sollat l'herba escapçada
surt algú de la casa poruc
i en veure'l surten els altres
tot fa pudor de fems, de cavall,
de tarda terriblement solitària.

19

the horses have galloped away
days ago they rose spirited
first one left and then the others
and the crushed grass, hoofprints
in the mud, the river muddied the grass beheaded
someone leaves the quaking house
and then the others see and leave
everything stinks of manure, of horse,
one afternoon terribly alone.

20

ets fecund, fecund, amor
i de tu faré un llarg intent
una nova melodia

20

you are bountiful, bountiful, love
and from you I will make a long composition
a new melody

21

plou
sobre el jardí adormit
lassa
la tardor
una fulla es sosté
entre el brancatge sec
cauen les gotes
una a una
cau la nit
i plou sobre el jardí
adormit

21

it's raining
on the sleeping garden
the afternoon
is tired
a leaf is caught
among the dry branches
drops fall
one by one
night falls
and it's raining on the garden
sleeping

22

cremen incendis
tot el poble piles fumejants
i els arbres rabiosos
de vermell
         de groc
               de grana

el foc llepa les fulles
llepa el cel
a cada cap de carrer
fogueres
atiades per homes gegants
de negres bigotis, negra pell

22

fires burn
the whole village smoking piles
and the rabid trees
of red
     of yellow
          of crimson

the fire licks the leaves
licks the sky
at the end of every street
bonfires
stirred by giant men
with black mustaches, black skin

23

hi ha una illa com un ull
erta sobre un mar impossible
una illa com un gran forat
per abocar-hi escumes, salives,
erecta cap a un cel distret
com un ressò, una explosió
l'illa com un forat
que refracta la llum
i enlluerna
res sinó una esponja gran
un eco, una presó
l'illa aquella
       o núvol

Ara un gran cor musculós
ressona per les cúpules celestes
l'illa les barnilles d'un cel gran
i vermellós
       com l'interior d'un home

23

there is an island like an eye
watchful over an impossible sea
an island like a great pit
where are poured foams, saliva,
straight up to a dreamy sky
like thunder, like an explosion
the island like a pit
that reflects light
and dazzles
nothing but a great sponge
an echo, a prison
this island
        or cloud

Now a big muscular heart
beats in the heavenly domes
the island the ribs of a vast sky
and red
        like the insides of a man

24

falseja
la veritable silueta de les coses
aquesta llum
el contorn d'un dia fi i polit
com un diamant
és una punxa, un gel
mentre els carrers continuïn desolats
tot – fins el plataner malalt –
deixa escaper unes llàgrimes
de metall fos àcids
que foradaran alguna cosa més
que el meu peu

per què tot no és sinó
una vaga idea que s'infla i s'infla
fins als límits del dolor
i no explota? per què el pes
de cada molècula ingràvida
no es deixa anar?
tu passes, i darrera teu
els carrers s'enfonsen
una gran esfera de pols
un anell, en un racó
brilla intrús una lluentor irreal

24

this light
falsifies the real
shapes of things
the outline of a day sharp and lovely
as a diamond
it's a spike, an ice cube
while the desolate streets run on
all – up to the sick palm tree –
tears escape
of metal melted to acid
that will bore a hole into more
than my foot

why is there nothing but
a vague idea that blows up and up
to the limits of misery
and doesn't explode? why isn't the weight
of every weightless molecule
just released?
you pass, and behind you
the streets collapse
a great sphere of dust
a ring, on a corner
an unreal glow intrudes

25

és una mà, una gran mà
damunt un cos més gran encara

translúcids ocells acabats de néixer
vagament intuïdors de la llum

freds corredors de la ciutat
què engoleixen?

com una ombra, la mà plana
damunt una ciutat indefensa
plena de llum

25

it's a hand, a big hand
on top of a body even bigger

translucent newborn birds
elusive prophets of light

cold city corridors
what do they swallow?

like a shadow, the flat hand
over a defenseless city
full of light

26

aquella papallona damunt el paviment
és una ombra xinesa, una cara
és un pensament
i de l'asfalt se'n desprèn cap al cel
una bombolla

al cel la fulla daurada
com un desig, un joc de mirades
gronxades pel vent

i aquí baix una basarda estremiment
quan el teu cos tremolós d'ales és
com una papallona

26

the butterfly on the pavement
is a Chinese shadow, is a face
is a thought
and a bubble frees itself from the asphalt
up to the sky

to the sky a gilded leaf
like desire, a game of glances
swaying in the wind

and here under a shudder of dread
when your body trembles with wings
like a butterfly

27

i un somriure allà al mig
mai ningú
no m'havia semblat tan bell
pujant
l'escala

27

and a smile right in the middle
nobody ever
seemed so beautiful to me
climbing
the stairs

Afterword

Maria-Mercè Marçal

I met Anna Dodas at the ceremony where she was awarded the Amadeu Oller Prize for her first book, *Landscape with Winter*. Not long after, we ran into each other again at a poetry reading in Lleida. These were the only two times I ever saw her. And yet I can't say that she was a stranger to me. Unlike those who knew her, knew her face, the sound of her voice, her gestures, her moods, and only later, perhaps, came to her poetry, I had the opposite experience. When I read the first lines of the first poem, I was starting from zero: I didn't have the predisposition we might have to the work of those close to us, either to be sympathetic or benevolent, or on the other hand, to be especially critical. Her poems came to me naked, and from the beginning they demanded my attention:

> Hair comes undone
> and stars shoot
> across a milky firmament.
> The acceleration, the jolt.
> My heart fits
> into the paw of an ogre.
> Gallop, gallop
> jump
> gallop, gallop
> mountains ferocious
> as the sea.

It's happened to me very few times, and this was one of them, that among the hundreds of poems you are obliged to read during the often tedious work as a member of a jury, there are poems that make you feel you will defend them fiercely, or even more, with no real or false modesty, as if they are poems of your own. I said to Anna, "These are poems I wish I'd written myself," and I meant it. From poet to poet, I don't know of higher praise.

And yet her poetic world is very personal and, as they say, non-transferable. A poetic world marked by desolation, closer to frightening than beautiful. The epigraph from Verdaguer with which she begins the collection says it well: "The tormented earth groans like a heart". We know by now that Anna seemed inclined to fiction and that her poetic outburst surprised more than a few of her friends. Maybe it was pain that brought her to poetry.

Though I know almost nothing more about her biography, by dint of her poems I can say that during the winter of 1985, she was deeply unhappy and depressed. It's true, I'm told, that it snowed incessantly. Anna converted this fact from reality into a continuing metaphor of her lived experience. The raw, white winter of 1985, with a countryside buried "beneath / the velvety marble slab" served for Anna Dodas both functions, perhaps predominantly the second. But also, surprisingly, in the midst of this deathly calm, "a brilliant meteor / frees itself / and lights the icy surface / of the earth." This "pulsating spark" turns round and round "like a chickpea / a ruby." And in the end is identified with blood, though an invulnerable blood, a hard blood, and so in a way already dead:

They must be very cold
much, much colder
to dissolve the mineral hardness
of fossilized
        blood.

In another poem, too, the important image from the first verse points to the love-death binary, and to anguish:

Horses came
with eyes of emerald.
A ring vivid green
surprised the night.
Death
strong in the saddle
and holding love
by the mane

To note again this absolute presence of death, the collection consists, and I think not arbitrarily, of thirteen poems. In the final one, suddenly:

Dawn rolls over
rumble of thunder.
It sounds, resounds
in the numb streets.

Curiously, the book *The Volcano* begins with a similar image:

I am like the groaning thunder
that roars in the valley
mad with terror

And it concludes, in the final poem that gives the book its title:

And the slender mountain
all alone and safe
carries thunder in her belly.

We don't need this insight, however, to realize the continuity between the two collections, though at first glance the titles seem anti-thetical. *Landscape with Winter* mimics in a certain manner the titles painters give to "still lifes," or to paintings where one element is super-imposed on another either without dissolving into the other. Landscape

with winter, it says, and not landscape of winter – which would be trite-
ly literal. Distance – even between the two elements of the title – cold,
stillness. Passivity. On the other hand, the connotations of "the volcano"
are absolutely opposite: activity, if only potential, the red of fire, lava,
thunder. Latent power and violence. This is very important:

> do you know what hides
> under the peaceful velvety
> green of the trees?
>   red

> what sucks the white
> flower, so it grows so fragile
> if not the fire?

I seem to hear in this poem an echo of the great North American poet
Emily Dickinson, only somewhat known among us, who said:

> On my volcano grows the Grass
> A meditative spot

> An acre for a Bird to choose
> Would be the General thought

> How red the Fire rocks below
> How insecure the sod
> Did I disclose would populate
> With awe my solitude.

And in another place:

> A still – Volcano – Life –
> That flickered in the night –
> When it was dark enough to do
> Without erasing sight –

152

Influence, coincidence? Either way: the idea is that of a latent violence, of a force that, on the outside, seems to have the fragility of a flower, or "the peaceful velvety green of the trees." Perhaps in essence it exudes the same constraint—despite the passage of time – of the archetypical feminine paradigm that now, just as in the 19th century, remains prevalent. A paradigm that excludes power, active force, from the notion of femininity. Contrary to this onus, a feminine voice that affirms itself in what we can call the "active" deed, the powerful deed, of writing. However, the powerful/powerless dialectic is permanent. The same poem that begins the book is, in this sense, strongly ambivalent. To the image of thunder – which, in any case, let us remember, was not the overpowering thunder of Zeus, but instead a "groaning" thunder "mad with terror" – in any case, to this image of "thunder," in essence violent and active in a way with which the poet identifies, follows another identification with a contradictory sign, basically receptive, concave:

I am the valley

But, again, an active image, that we can call phallic:

like a rake ...

This image too is mitigated by symbols of weakness:

like a rake
blind among the rocks
that stumbles on a clod of earth

But, at any rate, a rake: curiously, the same farm tool with which, in a tale by Víctor Català, a farm woman kills her rapist—a work tool that can become aggressive/defensive. There follows immediately a reverse image, very eloquent:

I am the channel ...

But this channel "dizzyingly" gushes water in a magnificent leap. And it concludes:

I am the leap

This vascillation between active/passive or receptive, strong/weak, powerful /powerless is most obvious, however, in the end, in the final lines, where desolation wins:

I am nothing more:
a wet poplar
that endures the rain
in misery

I have said that perhaps it was pain that brought Anna Dodas to poetry. Perhaps in every poet there is something of the anxious child humming to make it through a scary moment. Emily Dickinson said that she wrote poems as children sing when passing a cemetery: to ward off fear, the terror, so indistinct, without edges or railings, that is evil. When the galleys of this book came into my hands and I read it without a pause, I could not escape the idea that it was a premonition. Afterward I thought that with the hypersensitivity often bestowed by the gift of creativity, Anna had captured the dark, tragic core of reality. I believe this vision is related, not exclusively, but meaningfully, to her struggle with the reigning feminine archetypes. It is more perceptible in "the volcano" than in "the landscape with winter," and it takes a peculiar form in an impressive poem that, following in the footsteps of Sylvia Plath, she dedicates to her father. Sylvia Plath, another point of reference, perhaps, to locate the poetry of Anna Dodas. Perhaps, as Virginia Woof says, books "continue each other, in spite of our habit of judging them separately."

Anna's death was also the death of a woman in a hostile context. More than one sensible and well-meaning person, upon hearing the news, and after the first wave of outrage had passed, must have said: But, look, two

154

girls alone in the world ... As is the case for many poets who die tragically, the response to that kind of admittedly prudent comment is in one of her own verses:

nothing like fire, like the ember
and the hand that holds it and is burned ...

I seem to see in these verses the meaning – as if death can ever have a meaning – of her death. But what is literature, if not the attempt to give coherence and meaning to an amalgam of experiences and sensations that are essentially chaotic and fleeting ...

nothing like fire, like the ember
and the hand that holds it and is burned ...

In spite of the risk, and at a very high price, needless to say, Anna Dodas rejected "the agonizing succession of flames and incombustible days" and "the perverse powerlessness / of a fate that is nothing but waiting." These words, however, attest to the tension and the gamble. In spite of death, in this book we can still find her voice powerfully alive.

[Reprinted with permission of Heura Marçal from Maria-Mercè Marçal, *Sota el signe del drac: Proses 1985-1997*, Barcelona, Proa, 2004, 103-109.] Translated by Clyde Moneyhun